Krazy For Keto

Written by Brandon Kopp

ISBN: 979-8-9877118-0-4 (paperback)
979-8-9877118-1-1 (hardcover)

Book Cover and Illustrations by Zee
Book Design by Walton Burns

Country of Manufacture Specified on Last Page
First Printing 2023

To Mom, who helped me understand the diet and cooked countless meals for me.

To Dad, who researched treatments and found the Ketogenic Diet.

To my sister, Arielle, who ate her food in secrecy so I wouldn't be jealous.

Supporting The Charlie Foundation & Matthew's Friends

Ketogenic Dietary Therapies

Information • Training • Research • Support

A portion of the proceeds of this book will support the Children's Hospital
of Philadelphia Dietary Treatment Program
in the Division of Neurology

Brandon heard the school bell ring, and that meant it was finally time for summer!

When Brandon got home, his parents had a big surprise for him. They were going to the beach! Brandon was so excited because he loved the beach.

When they got to the beach, Brandon and his sister, Arielle, helped the family unpack, and Brandon was ready to start the fun!

Brandon swam in the ocean with his dad. They also went boogie boarding!

After a great time in the ocean, it was time for a snack.
Brandon and Arielle had some chips
and sandwiches waiting for them!

While Brandon was building a sandcastle,

he suddenly fell over. His mom and dad
ran to see what happened.

No matter what they tried, they couldn't get his attention.

His parents didn't know what happened, and they decided
that the best thing to do would be to call an ambulance.

The doctors told Brandon's parents
that Brandon had a seizure.

They would have to do more tests
to figure out what had caused it.

While in the hospital, Brandon had lots of visitors, and he got a bunch of stuffed animals and other toys to keep him occupied!

After having gone through many tests, Brandon was diagnosed with epilepsy and was sent home from the hospital with anti-seizure medicine. Brandon's family was hopeful that he wouldn't have any more seizures.

Brandon's parents wanted to keep him safe, so they took the doctor's recommendation and bought him a helmet to wear to protect his head in case he had more seizures and fell down.

Brandon didn't like the helmet at first, but then his parents let him decorate it with stickers from his favorite movies and games. Maybe it wouldn't be so bad after all. It wasn't uncomfortable, and he felt like a superhero wearing his special helmet!

When Brandon went to school with his new helmet, he was nervous about what his friends would say. He was scared they would make fun of him. But they didn't! It wasn't bad at all!

Back at home, Brandon didn't know how to swallow pills, so he would have to chew them. His mom tried to hide the bad flavor by mixing them with yogurt. Brandon hated both the taste of the medicine and how it made him feel.

Brandon's parents knew that they had to try something else to stop the seizures, so they found a new doctor who they hoped would help. The new doctor explained something called the Ketogenic Diet and how she thought it could help Brandon.

She said that maybe he could take less medicine or possibly even NO medicine! This made Brandon happy! Brandon's family discussed this option and decided to give it a try. They set a date to be admitted to the hospital to begin the diet.

The diet would mean getting rid of a lot of Brandon's favorite foods, but the doctor assured him that he would get to eat a lot of ice cream, whipped cream, and even hamburgers and hot dogs.

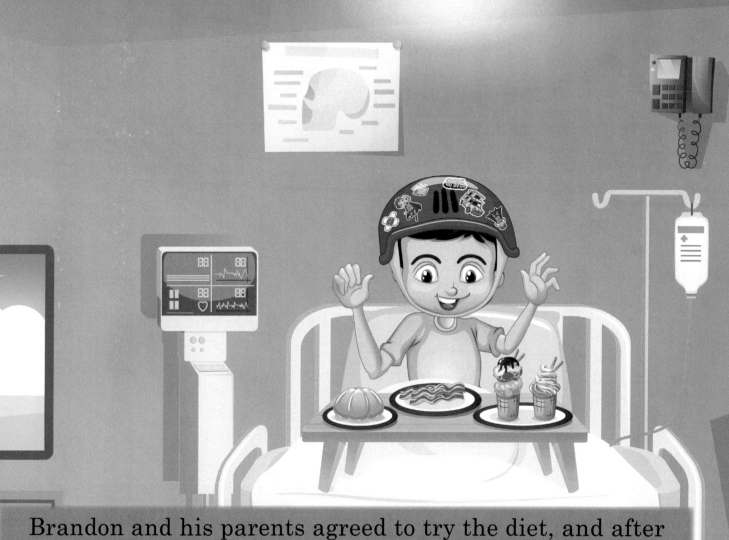

Brandon and his parents agreed to try the diet, and after spending a week in the hospital to get his body used to this new way of eating, Brandon was allowed to go home. The dietitian, the nurses, and the doctor all helped Brandon and his family learn about weighing food and figuring out his special meals. Brandon was now an official "Keto Kid!"

On his new diet, Brandon wouldn't have to take as much medicine, but he also couldn't eat the same types of food as he used to, which meant saying goodbye to some of his favorites. Bye bye waffles, pizza, and cereal. This was making Brandon a little sad.

But Brandon's parents made sure to make their own special food for Brandon. They got cookbooks and found recipes online. Brandon's mom put together a recipe book with pictures for Brandon to choose every meal that he wanted.

Sometimes Brandon was not a big fan of his meal.

When this happened, Brandon's mom would happily
give him other options!

Brandon's parents would keep track of what he liked to eat, and while there were some hard days, Keto was getting easier for Brandon day by day! The best part was that his seizures were going away, and he didn't have to wear a helmet anymore!

Sometimes Brandon was tempted to eat something he knew he wasn't supposed to. One time he saw a piece of cake on the kitchen counter. His parents were in another room, so he knew he could take it if he wanted to. But he never did because he understood it would be bad for him!

Brandon's desire for desserts and candy grew greater and greater as Halloween approached, but he didn't have much motivation to go trick or treating since he knew he couldn't eat any candy.

Thankfully, his parents thought ahead. They would give him a dime for every piece of candy he got! Brandon was excitedly counting his candy. Arielle decided to join him in trading her candy for money too!

Although he couldn't eat some of the same foods as before, Brandon realized how awesome Keto really was. As the months went on, he didn't have to take as much medicine as before he was a Keto Kid. He also didn't have to go to the hospital as often! Brandon was going Krazy for Keto!

Finally! After three years of being a Keto Kid and having no seizures, Brandon's doctor told him that he could start to eat more of his favorite foods!

Brandon and his family were so excited to attend this year's "Keto Kid" party at the hospital. He met some new friends and was happy to share with them his experience on the diet. They all agreed that it was really hard to do in the beginning, but then it got easier and easier.

One boy was so happy and told Brandon that he was still having a few seizures, but because they were mostly at night, he didn't have to wear a helmet anymore. Another girl said that she was excited to start the diet and was hoping to be able to take less medicine soon. A third little boy was thrilled that he was having no more seizures and was able to go back to school with his friends!

Brandon in the hospital after his first bout of seizures

Attending the National Walk for Epilepsy in Washington, D.C.

Brandon eating a keto pancake with cream

Hi, I'm Brandon! I've been off the Keto Diet for ten years (since 2012), and I haven't had a seizure since shortly after beginning the diet.

Thank you to my entire family and the Keto team at the Children's Hospital of Philadelphia for their support and encouragement during my time on the Ketogenic Diet.

I am forever grateful to my neurologist at the Children's Hospital of Philadelphia for first suggesting this amazing treatment and for helping me get through the difficult days! Although it was a challenging time for my entire family, everything I have today is only possible because of the Ketogenic Diet.

I would like to thank Jim and Nancy Abrahams for establishing the "Charlie Foundation," which has helped so many people around the world learn about this incredible treatment for retractable epilepsy.

I would also like to acknowledge Julie, Emma, and Matthew of "Matthew's Friends," which is helping to further spread the word about the Ketogenic Diet in the United Kingdom and beyond.

Although I am no longer on the Ketogenic Diet, it will be forever a part of my life. Since coming off the diet a decade ago, I have had the opportunity to meet with many families (both in person and on Zoom) who were just starting the diet. When I began hosting online meetings to help families from around the world connect with each other, I was often asked by the parents of new Keto Kids if I could recommend a book for their child to familiarize themselves with the diet. Since there were no such books available, I decided to write my story to help kids understand how the keto diet could make them better.

I really hope this book helps you and your family! You can read more of my story and get in touch with me at my website www. krazyforketo.org!

Thank you!

Brandon

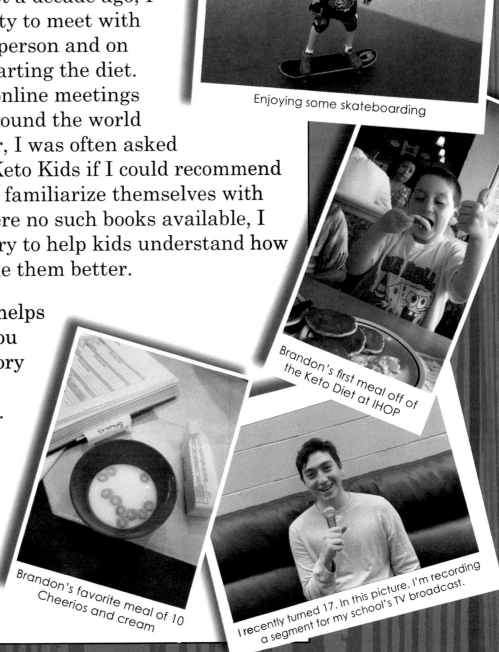

Enjoying some skateboarding

Brandon's first meal off of the Keto Diet at IHOP

Brandon's favorite meal of 10 Cheerios and cream

I recently turned 17. In this picture, I'm recording a segment for my school's TV broadcast.

Brandon is a 17-year old high school student who was diagnosed with a rare seizure disorder at the age of three. He was put on multiple anti-epilepsy medications, which not only did nothing to stop the seizures, but also came with a number of terrible side effects.

After consultations with several of the top pediatric neurologists in the United States, Brandon was put on the Ketogenic Diet for epilepsy. On day five of Brandon's hospital admission to begin the diet at the Children's Hospital of Philadelphia, his seizures stopped as abruptly as they started! Brandon did have several breakthrough seizures in the first two months after initiating the diet, but since then he has remained seizure-free.

After two and a half years on the diet, Brandon was successfully able to wean off all anti-seizure medicines and transition off the Ketogenic Diet. In the past seven years, Brandon has devoted much of his time to "paying it forward." He regularly meets with new Keto families and hosts Zoom meetings to connect them and answer their questions. During these meetings and other online forums, Brandon realized that parents were searching for resources to share with their children. Writing a children's book seemed like the perfect next step for Brandon.

Brandon is now a junior in high school where he is an honors student and involved in many extracurricular activities. In his free time, Brandon enjoys acting in school plays and performing Taylor Swift's discography in the shower!

Made in the USA
Middletown, DE
18 September 2023

38254789R00024